The Long Search
Story of Salman the Persian

Khurram Murad

The Islamic Foundation

© THE ISLAMIC FOUNDATION 1984/1404 H. Reprinted 1988/1408 H, 1994/1415 H and 2002/1423H.

ISBN 0 86037 137 9

MUSLIM CHILDREN'S LIBRARY

General Editors:
Khurram Murad and **Mashuq Ally**

THE LONG SEARCH

Author: **Khurram Murad**
Illustrations: **Hanife Hasan**
Editing: **Mardijah A. Tarantino**

These stories are about the Prophet and his Companions and, though woven around authentic ahadith, should be regarded only as stories.

Published by
THE ISLAMIC FOUNDATION,
Markfield Conference Centre,
Ratby Lane, Markfield,
Leicester LE67 9SY, United Kingdom
Tel: (01530) 244944/5, Fax: (01530) 244946
E-mail: i.foundation@islamic-foundation.org.uk
Web site: www.islamic-foundation.org.uk

QURAN HOUSE, P.O. Box 30611, Nairobi, Kenya

P.M.B. 3193, Kano, Nigeria

British Library Cataloguing in Publication Data

Murad, Khurram
    The long search – (Muslim children's library; 15)
    1. Muhammad (*Prophet*) – Juvenile literature
    I. Title II. Islamic Foundation III. Series
    297'.63 BP75

    ISBN 0-86037-137-9

MUSLIM CHILDREN'S LIBRARY

An Introduction

Here is a new series of books, but with a difference, for children of all ages. Published by the Islamic Foundation, books in the Muslim Children's Library have been produced to provide young people with something they cannot perhaps find anywhere else.

Most of today's children's books aim only to entertain and inform or to teach some necessary skills, but not to develop the inner and moral resources. Entertainment and skills by themselves impart nothing of value to life unless a child is also helped to discover deeper meaning in himself and the world around him. Yet there is no place in them for God, Who alone gives meaning to life and the universe, nor for the Divine Guidance brought by His prophets, following which can alone ensure an integrated development of the total personality.

Such books, in fact, rob young people of access to true knowledge. They give them no unchanging standards of right and wrong, nor any incentives to live by what is right and refrain from what is wrong. The result is that all too often the young enter adult life in a state of social alienation and bewilderment, unable to cope with the seemingly unlimited choices of the world around them. The situation is especially devastating for the Muslim child as he may grow up cut off from his culture and values.

The Muslim Children's Library aspires to remedy this deficiency by showing children the deeper meaning of life and the world around them; by pointing them along paths leading to an integrated development of all aspects of their personality; by helping to give them the capacity to cope with the complexities of their world, both personal and social; by opening vistas into a world extending far beyond this life; and, to a Muslim child especially, by providing a fresh and strong faith, a dynamic commitment, an indelible sense of identity, a throbbing yearning and an urge to struggle, all rooted in Islam. The books aim to help a child anchor his development on the rock of divine guidance, and to understand himself and relate to himself and others in just and meaningful ways. They relate directly to his soul and intellect, to his emotions and imagination, to his motives and desires, to his anxieties and hopes – indeed, to every aspect of his fragile, but potentially rich personality. At the same time it is recognised that for a book to hold a child's attention, he must enjoy reading it; it should therefore arouse his curiosity and entertain him as well. The style, the language, the illustrations and the production of the books are all geared to this goal. They provide moral education, but not through sermons or ethical abstractions.

Although these books are based entirely on Islamic teachings and the vast Muslim heritage, they should be of equal interest and value to all children, whatever their country or creed; for Islam is a universal religion, the natural path.

Adults, too, may find much of use in them. In particular, Muslim parents and teachers will find that they provide what they have for so long been so badly needing. The books will include texts on the Qur'ān, the *Sunnah* and other basic sources and teachings of Islam, as well as history, stories and anecdotes for supplementary reading. The books are presented with full colour illustrations keeping in view the limitations set by Islam. We invite parents and teachers to use these books in homes and classrooms, at breakfast tables and bedsides and encourage children to derive maximum benefit from them. At the same time their greatly valued observations and suggestions are highly welcome.

To the young reader we say: You hold in your hands books which may be entirely different from those you have been reading till now, but we sincerely hope you will enjoy them; try, through these books, to understand yourself, your life, your experiences and the universe around you. They will open before your eyes new paths and models in life that you will be curious to explore and find exciting and rewarding to follow. May God be with you forever.

May Allah bless with His mercy and acceptance our humble contribution to the urgent and gigantic task of producing books for a new generation of children, a task which we have undertaken in all humility and hope.

Khurram Murad
Director General

Our beloved Prophet Muhammad (Peace and Blessings be upon him)* once said: 'Salman is a member of my family.'

But Salman, in fact, was no relation to the Blessed Prophet. He was not even an Arab! So why did the Blessed Prophet say 'He is a member of my family'?

Abu Lahab, you may remember, was the Blessed Prophet's uncle. But instead of giving up the gods of stone and gods of wealth which he so greatly loved, and turning to the One Almighty God, he chose to oppose the Blessed Prophet in every way he could, so much so that he is the only one among the opponents of the Blessed Prophet whose name is cursed in the Quran.

As for the Blessed Prophet's parents, Abdullah and Amina, because they worshipped other gods besides the One God, he was not even allowed to ask forgiveness for them.

Yet Salman was considered a member of the Blessed Prophet's family. Who was he, then? Where did he come from?

*Muslims are required to invoke Allah's blessings and peace upon the Prophet whenever his name is mentioned.

In the days when the Blessed Prophet Muhammad had not yet become the Messenger of God, there lived in far-away Persia a small boy called Maduba. He was the only son in a wealthy family. His father was a man of high position and owned many acres of land near a little village outside of Isphahan, then the capital of Persia, now in Iran.

Now the little boy's father was a Zoroastrian. And a priest too. People of this religion worshipped fire. They believed they should be pure and of good character, and live clean lives. But they also believed that they had to worship fire, water and earth so that these elements would serve them well and cause them no harm. They did not understand that elements like fire are only creations of the One God, not the creators. Only One God rules over the whole world. Thus they made the great mistake of worshipping other gods besides the One God.

Maduba, whom we shall now call Salman, was also a very devout Zoroastrian, though he was still a young boy. Yet he was always eager to know the truth. He was also patient, and willing to endure great hardships.

Since he was the only son, his parents loved him greatly. As they were very wealthy, they spoiled him in every way they could. Every day, after his mother had bathed him and combed his long black locks the servants would dress him in fine silks and bring him every manner of delicious food. His father worshipped the very ground he walked on.

But what made him especially proud was when he discovered that his son took great joy in tending the Sacred Fire which burned by day and by night in the great central room of the house. Salman was very religious, so he was more than happy to assume the position of Qutan, keeper of the Sacred Fire. And since he did not have much else to do, he spent most of his time performing that task. By day and by night he sat in front of the blazing cauldron, carefully pouring on oil, and adding wood and bits of kindling.

His father, meanwhile, rejoicing in such devotion, loved him all the more, to such an extent that he could not bear to let him leave the house, and kept him inside just as if he were a girl. Time passed, and Salman continued to bask in the love of his parents without a care in the world. But one day something happened which was to change the course of his life.

'Salman, come here my dear boy', his father ordered one morning, and Salman came running.

'Listen closely. I have to get some urgent repairs done to the roof of the house or we shall have difficulties with rain and snow. I have no time to go to the fields and instruct the workers in what they should do today. You will have to help me. Ah! I do

not like to let you go like this, without you ever having been so far from home, but I have no other choice. Now listen carefully to what I say concerning the crops so that you can pass on my orders to the farmers.' When Salman's father had finished giving his instructions and he was sure Salman had understood them, he added 'Don't be late . . . and be sure to return before noon. I shall be waiting for you.'

Salman, once away from home, leapt for joy and went running down the path towards his father's fields, singing as he went. How marvellous it was to be outside in the open, away from the ever-present servants and the confines of the house!

How happy he was finally to have been given a responsible task to carry out.

As he went further and further away from home and approached the village, he heard, in the distance, the sweet sound of voices singing softly in unison. The hymns, for that is what they were, had an immediate effect upon Salman. He was so attracted to the sounds of worship that he took a side path, away from the direction he was going, towards the building from which the sounds came.

When he looked in the doorway he was surprised to see rows and rows of people standing, singing and kneeling. The beauty of it all touched him deeply. As soon as the singing was over he stopped the first person to approach him and began asking questions. He was told that their religion was called Christianity and they worshipped God. Time passed quickly as Salman stayed and listened to what the Christians had to say. Salman soon came to feel that Christianity was better than Zoroastrianism, that worshipping God was much closer to the truth than the worship of fire, air, earth or water.

When darkness began to fall, Salman realised that he had not gone to the fields as his father had ordered him to do. What could he do? Quickly he bade farewell to the Christians and ran home as fast as he could.

Salman's father was frantic. He had sent out the servants to search for his son, but they had come back without news of him. He was pacing the floor when Salman entered the house. Seeing his son, he rushed forward to embrace him; but his face turned dark when he heard about Salman's visit to the Christian church. He became even more upset when Salman told him that the Christian religion seemed much closer to the truth than the worship of fire.

'The true God must be the one who created everything, isn't that so, father?' asked Salman. 'I feel in my heart that their way of worship is the right one for me.'

His father became very upset. 'How can you say such a thing? Have you forgotten all I have taught you? Have you forgotten the sacred fire, the rites and duties which you have faithfully followed?'

He turned away, overwhelmed with emotion. He was hurt that his son should be willing to disobey him and frightened lest this bring misfortune upon his household. Why did he ever let his son out of the house? He had been right, all these years, to keep him close by, and he should have continued to do so.

'Never again shall I let you out', he said with bitterness, 'I must keep you at home. I cannot risk you meeting these people again. Remember that fire is pure. Through fire you can be purified. This is the way of our forefathers and this should be your way too. Anything else is a lie.'

And so saying, he ordered his servants to bolt the gates and to keep a close watch on Salman, chaining his feet at night, if need be.

But Salman did not lose heart. He did not protest because he understood why his father was acting in this way, though it made him very sad.

Finally, one night when he was chained in his room, a very dear old servant came to see him. 'Please', Salman whispered, 'you say you have .loved me since I was a baby. Now I ask you, show me your love by carrying this message for me to the church people in the village. That is all I ask of you.' The old servant agreed and blessed his young master, as he left to deliver the message.

Salman's plan was to catch a trade caravan heading towards the central area of the Christian religion, which he had been told was in Syria. The church people, he hoped, would let him know when that caravan would come through. Even though Salman was young and inexperienced, his heart was firm and he was sure of his new faith. Moreover, his desire to seek the truth was greater than whatever fear he had of the unknown.

Eventually, one night, the old servant crept into Salman's room and woke him. 'Master', he whispered, 'I have heard from the church people. They say a caravan will pass through the village at midnight tonight. They say you should leave immediately.'

The servant wept as he unlocked the boy's chains, and wished him good luck and blessings on his journey.

'Thank you, old man', replied Salman. 'Please let me have your cloak so no one will recognise me.'

The next morning, when Salman's parents discovered that he had gone, they were frantic. They

SYRIA

Mosul

ISFAHAN

Persian Gulf

• Al Qura

• Madina

Red Sea

sent search parties everywhere, but the caravan bearing Salman had long gone, and no one had seen him join it. The old servant, true to his word, kept silent about the whole matter.

Salman was now on the first leg of his long journey in search of the truth.

When at last he arrived in Syria, he went immediately to the first church he saw, and spoke to the people there. He was surprised at their kindness, and at how patiently they listened to him. After giving him refreshments they directed him to the bishop of the town.

'Your Grace', he said, 'I have left my home in search of the truth. The Christian religion seems to me much closer to the truth than the worship of fire, which is the only religion I know. I would like to know more about your religion. If you would allow me, sir, I would like to be your servant and tend to your needs and the needs of the church, and in turn I would be able to learn the rituals and prayers of the Christian religion.'

The people around smiled at the boy, while the bishop nodded in agreement at the proposal and seemed most anxious to have Salman as his servant. What Salman did not know was that the bishop was especially glad to have someone work for him without pay!

At first Salman was more than grateful for his new position. During the day he kept house for the bishop, polished the altar pieces, swept the church and served meals. At night, he would pray and learn the rituals of the church.

But as time went by, Salman noticed things which shocked him. He began to realise that the bishop was a hypocritical man, friendly and smiling with members of his congregation, then mocking them behind their backs. And worse still, he accepted from them generous contributions, meant for the poor, but instead of seeing that they were distributed to those in need, he would pocket the money and spend it on himself or add it to the brimming coffers of gold and silver which he kept locked away.

Salman could hardly believe what he saw. He tried to concentrate all his attention on his prayers, but his repugnance of the bishop's behaviour would not leave him in peace. He kept trying to remember that he had become a Christian not for the sake of a bishop but for the sake of the truth. 'If this man is committing sin, it is no concern of mine. He will be punished according to just merit by Almighty God in due time. As for me, I shall continue striving to perfect myself in my new religion', said Salman to himself.

One day, quite suddenly, the bishop was stricken with fever and died. When the news of his death spread, there was great sorrow throughout the city. The Christians began to assemble from near and far for the burial service, mourning and bewailing the loss of their great religious leader. Sorrow was in their faces and in their hearts, and everyone was consoling everyone else.

But Salman was seething with anger. He would seek the first opportunity to tell the people the truth about their bishop. He waited until everyone was assembled for the burial service, when he could restrain himself no longer.

Mounting the altar platform he called for their attention.

'Good people, I must tell you the truth. Your bishop was a fraud! He exhorted you to charity, but he used all the money you donated for his own needs, or hoarded it in the coffers which he kept for that purpose. He never gave away one penny to the poor!'

The people were completely taken aback by such an accusation.

'This is blasphemy!' 'Ungrateful foreign wretch . . . ' 'He is lying!' some cried. But at the same time, they knew that Salman had been living in the church house and had been close to the bishop every day for months. They simply could not disbelieve him.

'How do you know this?' they asked. 'Show us some proof, if what you say is true!'

'If it is proof you want, then follow me', answered Salman.

He led them down a narrow corridor and stopped before a heavy wooden door. Loosening a brick from the wall, he took out a polished iron key which had been hidden behind it, unlocked the massive door, and pushed it open. Everyone rushed in. There, before their eyes were seven huge coffers overflowing with gold and silver and ornaments. These were all the riches which the congregation, over many years, had donated for the poor!

Realising the truth of Salman's words they became outraged. They rushed to seize the body of the bishop and, while Salman watched helplessly, hauled it to the village square where they hanged and stoned it.

So it was that the bishop's punishment began even before he was to meet his Maker.

Weeks went by, and then the congregation installed another bishop as their religious leader. Salman soon discovered that this new bishop was a truly pious man. He sought nothing of this world, but was always doing good deeds in the hope that he might be rewarded by Almighty God in the Hereafter. He spent nights and days in prayer with the faithful

Salman always at his side. Great love grew between them until one day, the bishop realising that he was soon to die, called Salman to his side.

'My son, I am dying. Do not linger here, you must go to the city of Mosul and there, I know, is a good Christian man who will take care to instruct you as I have tried to do . . . God be with you, my son . . . ', and with these words, the bishop passed away.

In deep mourning, for the man who had cared for him when he was so much in need, Salman officiated at the services of the church for the last time.

Then, following the bishop's instructions, he set off for Mosul.

The second stage of Salman's journey was to be a most unusual time for him. During these years he was to meet with three more bishops, each of them a sincere, pious Christian to whom he became very attached and who, in turn, came to love him too.

After the death of the Syrian bishop, Salman went to join the Bishop of Mosul with whom he stayed for many years as a servant and companion. Before his death, the bishop advised Salman to go to Nassibayn, and then, when the Bishop of Nassibayn came to the end of his life, he instructed Salman to go to Ammuriyya. Each time, Salman told the story of his search, his desire to discover the truth, and of his wish to become a servant of God. And with each bishop he was welcomed and invited to prove the sincerity of his intentions to his new patron.

During these years, Salman grew in maturity and became more and more convinced that there is but One God and that the elements, earth, fire and water, which his ancestors had held sacred, were but creations of the One Creator, just as he himself was. He knew he was on the right path. But had the path come to an end?

In later years, Salman was to look back upon the extraordinary chain of events in his life which were to lead him to his goal.

Arriving at Ammuriyya, Salman recounted his story yet again, and was immediately taken in by the bishop who soon developed great trust and affection for the boy.

Once again, Salman tended the altar, polished the heavy metal pieces and prepared the clean linen for the mass; then he helped by mending the bishop's clothes and tending to all his personal needs. When he was not so occupied, he spent every free moment in prayer and worship, sometimes by himself in his bare cell, sometimes with the bishop, through the long hours of the night. By day he studied the Christian religion and learned the scriptures.

The bishop had such confidence in Salman, that he suggested the young man broaden his knowledge and learn to attend to the practical things of life as well. In order to help him, he gave Salman a plot of land and some cows and goats. 'This is also the work of the Lord', he said, 'for everything in creation belongs to Him'.

But the old bishop's health was failing. He often neglected his own comfort, and as a result caught a chill one night, which got steadily worse in spite of Salman's efforts to cure him. Finally, one evening he called to the youth in a feeble voice:

'My dear boy, I am not long on this earth. In these last days, I have been thinking of what shall become of you once I am dead.'

Salman's heart sank as he heard these words. Was he to lose, yet again, a dear friend and benefactor? But the bishop, to Salman's astonishment, seemed to be looking far into the distance and smiling. 'I have prayed that I might, in my last hours, be able to guide you to what you have been seeking for so long. My prayer has been answered. I have something to tell you which should relieve you of any worry about your future. For I feel that, no matter what trials and tribulations you may encounter, you will, one day, meet the last of the Prophets . . . the Prophet who has been clearly foretold in our scriptures . . . '

Salman was astounded by these words, but kept silent so as not to interrupt. The old man motioned for water, and Salman dutifully moistened his lips.

'I have not told you before' continued the old man, 'of that Prophet. He will come from Arabia and will bring men to a purer and nobler life . . . listen carefully . . . after living for a while in his home city, he will receive God's message and call people to the worship of the One God alone. Some will leave aside their evil ways of idol worship and sin, and follow him. But, as a result, his enemies will force him to leave that city and he will have to move to another one . . . a city which is located between two black hills where there are groves of date palms. Remember, my son! Two black hills . . . '

Salman nodded and repeated 'two black hills'. 'But', he added, a bit dismayed and puzzled, 'how shall I know this man when I see him? How shall I recognise him?'

'There are signs . . . ' murmured the old bishop, 'there are many signs, but for you there will be three . . . listen closely', and he beckoned Salman to come nearer. 'If you offer him charity, he will not accept it; that is the first sign.

The second is this: if you offer him a gift, he will accept it.

The third sign is the birthmark: between his shoulder-blades he bears the birthmark which is the

Seal of Prophethood.

By these three signs you shall know who he is.'

The bishop remained silent for several minutes, then, raising his hand towards Salman, with his last dying breath he blessed him, and passed away.

Salman shed many tears after the bishop's death. But behind his grief was the memory of the bishop's smile, and the promise that one day he, Salman, would meet the man sent by God. His whole being yearned for that one thing, to meet the last of the Prophets and to live by his side.

After a while, a trade caravan from Arabia led by people of the Kalb tribe, came through the town. Salman, seeing his opportunity, rushed to greet them and told them that he wanted to join them on their journey back to Arabia. With wicked smiles, the men eyed this innocent young man. 'What will you pay us, eh? We do not give free rides, boy', they said scornfully.

Salman did not hesitate. 'Take what I have . . . take my cows and my goats, everything . . . but you must take me with you.' This, of course, is exactly what they wanted.

So Salman joined the caravan, and with each day grew more and more excited as they approached Arabia. The men he was travelling with were rude

and coarse, but Salman paid no attention to them. He was preoccupied with his own dreams and prayers, and his hopes for the future.

Finally, one day, they reached the Valley of al-Qura, which is located between Syria and Madina. They had stopped to tend the camels and rest, when Salman noticed some people approach the caravan and address the leader. They began talking amongst themselves and seemed to be haggling over the price of something. Finally the caravan leader, who had been handed a money purse by the strangers, headed in Salman's direction.

'Your journey's over, my innocent friend', he laughed, grabbing Salman from behind. 'Time to join these nice people here', he added, pushing Salman towards the strangers, who shackled his ankles and led him off.

It was too late to flee. 'Alas, what has become of me! I have been sold into slavery to the people of this settlement. Only God knows how far away from the city of date-palm groves and of two black hills', moaned Salman to himself. Letting his head drop, he tried to summon up a Prayer for his safety.

At dawn the next day he was led to the date gardens and told he would have to work all day in the hot sun until evening. He was given only a small amount to eat and drink, but to Salman it didn't matter, as he

was used to living on very little. What he suffered from most was that he felt so alone, so helpless. How would he be able to find his teacher now? What chance did he have of escaping his fate?

There was only one thing left for him, and that was prayer. There was nothing else to do, no one to turn to save the One God. It was at those times, during the lonely, dark nights as he lay on his straw mat, that he realised how fortunate he was to have been shown the gift of prayer. He prayed: 'Dear God! Please deliver me from this suffering. Let me find the true path. Lead me to the last of the Prophets. Deliver me from bondage, and lead me to freedom. Amin.'

Whenever he uttered these words to himself, a feeling of calm, like cool water, flowed over him. His anguish and sadness disappeared. In its place, he felt peace such as he had witnessed on the face of the old bishop when he took his last breath.

One day his master hastened up to him. 'You have been sold to my cousin', he announced. 'You are leaving this afternoon for Yathrib where you will work for him.'

To Salman it did not make much difference which man he belonged to, since he was no longer his own master. Nor did he care where they were going. What did it matter whose slave he was? What did it matter where he lived, since it was not of his choice? Salman paid no attention to the direction they took, nor to the surrounding countryside. He just stumbled on behind his master, led by his shackled wrists which were beginning to pain him.

At one point he stumbled, and as he raised himself he saw, in the distance, a sight which made his heart leap with joy. There they were! To the north and to the south of him, two black hills! And in front of him, a short distance away, a grove of date palms. Could this be it? Surely this must be the city of the black hills, for there they were! Surely here he would meet, after all this time, after all this searching, sacrifice and suffering, the new prophet which the bishop had told him about!

Salman raised himself to his full height and walked, now, lightly and with joy, so that his master, seeing the sudden change in his slave, wondered about it and kept a close eye on him.

Nothing much else happened to Salman in the days that followed. His life was a monotonous one, filled with hard work and little food. Still, he did not mind, for when he awoke at dawn each morning, he saw before him the two black hills, and around him the date groves. These were the reminders of his search. Symbols of hope for him every minute of the day, so that his heart became filled with patience and eagerness at the same time.

Yes, he would be patient now. He was sure that the Blessed Prophet would come to this very city, and had he but known the truth, his feeling was correct.

The Blessed Prophet's days in Makka were coming to an end. Torture and persecution by the Makkans forced him to leave the city and depart in search of a new place from where to carry on his mission. The direction of his departure was towards the city of Yathrib, now known as Madina.

One day, Salman was working in the gardens, up one of the date trees, when someone came rushing towards his master, who was sitting in the shade below him.

'A curse be on all of us!' cried the man. 'Have you heard the news?'

Salman's master got up and went towards his colleague. 'What's happened now?' he asked.

'That trouble-maker from Makka is moving to our city! The Aus and the Khazraj have invited him here along with his whole band of followers. What did I tell you? When those foreigners began moving in it was going to lead to some kind of trouble. They say this so-called prophet and his followers from Makka are staying at Quba and they are planning to march right into our town! The Aus and the Khazraj are fools who don't know what they're getting themselves into.'

'Hmmph!' commented Salman's master. 'We don't need any new prophets, least of all one who is hated in his home city!'

Salman, perched high up in the tree, began to tremble with emotion. The Jew's words had struck him to his very soul. He sat there, unable to breathe, and for a moment thought he would lose his grip on the tree and fall down on his master, but he held on until he could control himself. Then he climbed down and stood before the two men.

'What are you saying?' he demanded. 'Who is this man from Makka, what do they call him?'

His master was outraged at this impertinence. He slapped Salman's face and kicked him. 'What has this got to do with you? Go back to work and don't meddle with what does not concern you. Remember your place, you are only a slave!' he shouted.

When evening came, Salman could wait no longer. Throwing caution to the winds, he gathered together his ration of dates and made his way through the dark streets and down the mountain path to the little town of Quba, where he had heard the Blessed Prophet was staying. It was already late when he entered the town and sought directions. It seemed that everyone knew where the Blessed Prophet was to be found.

As he entered the house, he saw before him a handsome man with huge dark eyes and a gentle smile. Salman's heart began to beat as he moved forward to meet him.

'Sir', he said, 'I know that you have just arrived from Makka and that there are others travelling with you.'

The Blessed Prophet nodded and waited for Salman to continue.

'I have some dates with me . . . ' and Salman produced a packet from his bag, ' . . . which I have been intending to give to charity. Please be so kind as to accept them.

The Blessed Prophet looked at him intently for a moment and then smiled, and Salman noted that there was kindness in his eyes. Taking the dates from Salman, he proceeded to pass them out to his Companions who were sitting around him in the room. 'Please . . . eat!' he urged. But Salman noticed that the Blessed Prophet did not take even one date for himself. 'He has passed the first test', said Salman to himself. 'He has refused charity for himself, as the bishop said he would', and Salman retired to a corner of the room to ponder on what had happened.

Salman stayed quite late that evening, listening to the Blessed Prophet and his followers make plans for the future. Finally, Salman realised that it was getting late and that he would have to hurry back before his master discovered his absence, so he excused himself and promised to return another time.

Salman wondered when he would be able to return to Quba. He had managed to sneak away once, but how would he ever make such a journey a second time without raising his master's suspicions?

A few days later, as he was following his master to the gardens, they met with great excitement on the road. A large procession appeared, led by a man on a white camel. Salman couldn't be sure, but he thought he recognised the Blessed Prophet and his followers.

'Hmmph', grumbled his master to himself. 'Here they come, the whole lot of them. That self-made prophet should have found some place else to move to instead of disturbing our peaceful town.'

So the Blessed Prophet had moved to Madina! That night, having learned that he was staying in the house of Abu Ayub al-Ansari, Salman gathered some dates and made his way there as fast as he could.

A crowd of people were milling around the doorway and there was great excitement. Salman moved through the crowd and approached the Blessed Prophet. He spoke in a bold voice, but inside he was trembling with anxiety.

'Sir', he said, 'I noticed the other night when I

offered you some dates as charity that you yourself ate none of them. Perhaps you will accept these as a present?'

Once again the Blessed Prophet looked at Salman with kindness and affection, and thanked him for the present. Carefully, he chose one date, ate it, and passed the others to his Companions.

Salman breathed a sigh of relief and retreated behind the crowd to be by himself. 'So', he nodded to himself, 'this prophet has accepted for himself a present but he did not eat of a charity; this was the second test'. Already, in his heart, Salman was beginning to feel that this was the man whom the bishop had been talking about. Everything in his manner, in the way he moved and spoke to people, even to the chance meeting on the road, pointed to it. Yet still, he had to be certain.

The following evening, when Salman came to Abu Ayub's house, a circle of men were gathered to say Prayers for the dead. Salman looked around but saw no altar pieces nor linen. 'With what do you worship God?' he asked of a follower. 'With what God gave us', answered the other, 'with our bodies and our voices'.

'And where is your priest, your intermediary?'

'We need no one to intercede. Allah hears our prayers', was the answer. Salman was astounded and impressed. He could never have imagined a religion so simple, so direct. As he listened to the passages of Ya Sin, his being was filled with a feeling of worship:

' . . . It is a revelation
Sent down by Him
The Exalted in Might,
Most Merciful,
In order that thou mayest
Warn a people,
Whose fathers had received
No warning, and who
Therefore remain heedless
Of the Signs of God . . . '

When the Prayers were over, Salman moved forward to greet the Blessed Prophet, and then chose a place to sit directly behind him. The Blessed Prophet was wearing his turban for the occasion, and a loose garment over his shoulders. If the Blessed Prophet turned slightly, Salman might be able to see if he had the Seal of Prophethood between his shoulder blades.

After a while, the Blessed Prophet became conscious of someone sitting behind him staring at his back. He turned and saw Salman, and at that moment must have understood what it was Salman was looking for, for he let slip his garment ever so slightly.

When Salman saw with his own eyes the Seal, he

burst into uncontrollable sobs of gratitude and joy.

The Blessed Prophet put his arm around Salman and asked gently: 'What is the matter, my son? What moves you so much?'

The followers stopped talking to one another and looked up to see who was sobbing and what the Blessed Prophet was saying.

Salman dried his tears and tried to calm himself. Then, encouraged by the Blessed Prophet, he told, little by little, the story of his long search.

Finally he said: 'Every sign the bishop told me about you has been confirmed. And now that I am here, please allow me to join your religion of Islam, the worship of the One God, which I am convinced is the truth I have been searching for.'

The Blessed Prophet nodded and seemed very happy with Salman's story.

Many years later, when Salman was to tell about this wonderful day, he said: 'They were all so surprised by my story and showed such delight at my wish to join Islam.'

Salman was now filled with joy and enthusiasm. But he knew that in order to be a constant companion of the Blessed Prophet he would have to free himself from slavery. How was he to do that? He wondered about his future since he could think of no way to change his fate.

The Companions, meanwhile, were determined to help Salman, whom they loved very much. Eventually they thought up a plan whereby they were quite certain Salman's Jewish master would release him from slavery. Calling Salman aside, they said to him:

'Listen to us, brother, and do not interrupt nor refuse our plan. You should be free from slavery, you know, therefore you must follow our advice.'

Salman listened while they told him what to do, and they handed him 40 ounces of gold which they had collected from the Muslim community. Salman was so touched that he did not know what to say and tried to refuse the gift, but the Companions insisted.

The next day, he approached his master.

'Sir', he began. 'You know that I desire to gain my freedom. I have here 40 ounces of gold which I shall give you. Will you release me from slavery?'

The gold was much more than what his master could expect. He thought it over and decided that it was not at all a bad idea. But, perhaps, he could extract more, especially if Salman's newly-found friends were so keen to gain his freedom and so helpful. So he said: 'Alright, I agree. First, hand over the gold.

But besides that, you will plant 300 date trees, and the day they begin to bear fruit you will be released from my bondage. Is this agreeable to you?'

'Three hundred date trees won't all blossom in one year', he reasoned to himself. 'I'll get a few more years of work out of him yet.'

The following day the whole Muslim community went out in the fields to plant the date trees. Salman was surprised when the Blessed Prophet himself came to help plant the trees and to bless each one as it was put into the ground.

Perhaps it was because of his blessing that all the trees, that very same year, began to bear fruit.

The Jew was astonished. 'To tell you the truth, Salman, I never expected 300 trees to all bear fruit so soon! I thought to keep you a while longer in my service!'

And so, reluctantly, he gave Salman his freedom, and everyone in the Muslim community rejoiced at the outcome. 'Praise Allah', they cried, and prepared a little feast to mark the occasion. The Blessed Prophet attended the feast, and as it was about to begin, he took up a few dates in his hand. 'Salman', he said, 'eat of these dates from me, and Allah will bless you!' Salman took the dates with many thanks.

That year there were many friendly arguments amongst the Companions. The question was whether Salman was a Muhajir, an immigrant, or an Ansar, a helper from Madina.

The Muhajirs argued: 'Obviously Salman is one of us! He comes all the way from Persia; if that is not an immigrant, we would like to know what is!'

The Ansars, the helpers from Madina, countered with much indignation: 'Salman, an immigrant? Of course not. He was already living in Madina when the Blessed Prophet moved here . . . he was here before you came. So of course he is an Ansar, one of us!'

But the Blessed Prophet had something to say about it. 'Salman', he declared, 'is a member of my family'.

And as for Salman himself, with deep devotion and thanksgiving he declared: 'I am Salman, a son of Islam.'